MW01384418

# *Miss Caledonia*

# Miss Caledonia

Melody A. Johnson

*Miss Caledonia*
first published 2013 by
Scirocco Drama
An imprint of J. Gordon Shillingford Publishing Inc.
© 2013 Melody A. Johnson

Scirocco Drama Editor: Glenda MacFarlane
Cover photo by Rick Roberts
Cover design by Terry Gallagher/Doowah Design Inc.
Author photo by Richard Burdett
Printed and bound in Canada on 100% post-consumer recycled paper.

We acknowledge the financial support of the Manitoba Arts Council and The Canada Council for the Arts for our publishing program.

All rights reserved. No part of this book may be reproduced, for any reason, by any means, without the permission of the publisher. This play is fully protected under the copyright laws of Canada and all other countries of the Copyright Union and is subject to royalty. Changes to the text are expressly forbidden without written consent of the author. Rights to produce, film, record in whole or in part, in any medium or in any language, by any group amateur or professional, are retained by the author.
Production inquiries should be addressed to:
Tammy Fox
The Collection Agency Entertainment
(905) 372-6161
www.thecollectionagency.ca

Library and Archives Canada Cataloguing in Publication

Johnson, Melody A.
Miss Caledonia / Melody A. Johnson.

A play.
ISBN 978-1-897289-84-6

I. Title.

PS8619.O4825M58 2013 C812'.6 C2013-900584-6

J. Gordon Shillingford Publishing
P.O. Box 86, RPO Corydon Avenue, Winnipeg, MB Canada R3M 3S3

# Acknowledgements

Sheryl Baraniuk, Suzanne Belanger, Blyth Festival, Rich Burdett, Marjorie Campbell, Kyle Capstick, The Coles, John and Lois Douglas, Jane Douglas, Melanie and David Douglas, Claire Ross Dunn, Jacqui Good and Leon Cole, The Grand Theatre, Amy Henkel, Eda Holmes, Gregory Hoskins, Humber College, Jane Johanson, Ann Marie Kerr, Lighthouse Festival, Tammy Fox, Andy McKim, Chris Oldfield, Ontario Arts Council, Devon Potter, Richard Rose and the Tarragon Theatre staff, Summerworks, David Talbot, Julie Tepperman, Toronto Arts Council, Megan Vaudry, and Eric Woolfe. And of course farmers and their families everywhere.

# Playwright's Note

*Miss Caledonia* is based on the true story of my extraordinary mother Peggy Johnson (nee Douglas). I was so intrigued by the notion of using pageants to escape the farm—as so many teenage gals did in the 1950's—that I couldn't resist writing about it.

The Douglas farm on Rural Route 2, Caledonia is still in full swing these days, operated by John Douglas, Peggy's younger brother. The log cabin was dismantled and sold to a Toronto buyer in 1962 to be rebuilt for museum purposes. A new and perfectly level home now stands on the premises.

Countless biographies and autobiographies of movie and stage stars fueled my mother's passion for the art of entertainment. Her many batons, sashes, trophies and pageant outfits remain a part of our lives today, each one a remembrance of a great period of celebration and excitement of what could be. This play is dedicated with great love and admiration for Peggy / Mom.

—Melody A. Johnson

## Production History

*Miss Caledonia* was originally presented for the 2010 Toronto Summerworks Festival at the Factory Theatre Studio, followed by presentations at the Lighthouse Theatre, Blyth Festival, and the Grand Theatre. The full 75-minute version as written here premiered at the Tarragon Theatre, Toronto, on Oct 13, 2012 with the following cast and crew:

Written and Performed by Melody A. Johnson

Directed by Rick Roberts and Aaron Willis

Musical Direction and Accompaniment: Alison Porter

Lighting Design by Raha Javanfar

Stage Manager: Jessica Severin

## Set

*Miss Caledonia* is a memory play told to us through narrator Peg Douglas. Peg jumps back and forth in time revisiting the many friends, family and creatures who inhabited her youth in rural southern Ontario, in and around 1955. Because this is a memory play, it is not naturalistic, and therefore there are no props or costumes. There is a lone bench centre stage which transforms throughout the piece. A fiddler occasionally adds to the environment and often prods, cautions, and cheers on our narrator.

## Melody A. Johnson

Melody has performed from Brantford to Singapore, and has created many characters in the Canadian theatre canon, including Jason Sherman's *It's All True*, Claudia Dey's *Trout Stanley*, Florence Gibson's *I Think I Can*, and Colleen Murphy's *The Piper*. Other favourite roles include characters in *7 Stories* (Theatre Calgary/CanStage, Betty Mitchell award nomination), *In the Next Room* (Tarragon/MTC), *Our Town* (Two Planks and a Passion, Merritt Award nomination), *Blithe Spirit* (Soulpepper), *Habeus Corpus* (Canstage), and *The Seven Lears* (Swollen Tongues).

Melody is an alumna of The Toronto Second City mainstage where she has directed the National Touring Company, and *0% Down*, *Second City for Mayor*, and *We've Totally Probably Got This*. Comedic turns include *An Awkward Evening with Martin & Johnson* with fellow alum Bob Martin (*The Drowsy Chaperone*). Melody has received numerous Dora nominations, and won for the title role of Mercy in Morwyn Brebner's *Little Mercy's First Murder* (Tarragon/Shaw Festival).

In addition to writing and acting in *Miss Caledonia*, Melody co-created the musical *Mimi* with Rick Roberts and Allen Cole for the Tarragon Theatre in 2009.

Melody resides in Toronto with her husband and composer Allen Cole and their lovely son Dashiell Douglas Cole.

For more information, visit melodyjohnson.ca

# Act I

## Prologue

*FIDDLER enters stage left into small pool of light. She sits and begins to play a kind of water soundscape. Blackout. A moment later lights up centre on a forty-something PEG. She stands for a beat and then…*

PEG: I read somewhere that when you're about to crash yer vehicle on the highway yer heart pounds at an accelerated rate, causin' you to shake and discombobulate, yer adrenalin pumps an' thumps' through ya, your vision's momentarily screwed up an you lose all sense o' time an' place.

*Light shift to stark brightness on PEG.*

AHHHHH!

*Light shifts back to warmer spot on PEG, and back up on FIDDLER.*

Winning a beauty pageant is like that. Losing a beauty pageant's like that too, only the end part's less pretty.

In the spring of 1955 it seemed like the rain would never stop. Everything looked an' smelled like worm soup; which is not good news when you rely on the land.

*Beat. FIDDLER stops water soundscape.*

Mom, Dad'n me, we lived here on rural route

two, Caledonia, ten miles east of Brantford, six miles south of Hamilton. County of Haldimand. Population sign read 2,015. It was really about 2,008, since both the Stewarts and the Wilsons decided to move to the big city but nobody had the inclination to change the sign.

*Beat.*

We lived right here on Highway 54, some people called it Douglas Road I spose because there were so many of us dottin' the landscape at that time. An' everybody knew everybody else. We all knew who was Liberal an' who was Anglican. And o' course we all went to church so we also knew who could sing an' who couldn't.

*Fiddle plays, almost turning PEG upstage to survey her surroundings.*

This was our ol' log house. Dad paid about thirty nine hundred in 1938. Built by the Indians Dad said. Pine tongue and groove, quarter inch thick made from trees on the land. Y'ever see a steeper slope than this? More crooked than a banker on a Tuesday. You put an egg here in this west corner, let go, it'd roll faster than you can say "Massey Ferguson".

Mom papered the back kitchen there with newspaper, she had the good sense to paper it with good news from 1917, 1918 'bout the war endin', women gettin' the vote that kind o' thing. Mom an' Dad's back bedroom's there, this here'd be our living room—

*FIDDLER makes windmill sound prodding PEG to turn and look.*

An' right out that west window's our nice tall, steel windmill, always seemed to be watchin' over us all in its' own majestic kind o'way. Slight wind today; seems like it can't make up its mind which way to turn. And right over there, past them three tall sunflowers lookin' like widows, that'd be our… outhouse.

*Fiddle sting of darkness.*

Our sole source of intestinal relief, a full 180 years past the invention of the flush toilet.

An' in 1955, at fifteen, I was like a mouse in a maze desperately searchin' for a way out of the lopsided, bathroomless, chickory-pullin' life I was livin'. Then I heard about this little farm gal from El Paso Texas named Mary Frances Reynolds who won the Miss Burbank beauty pageant at fifteen, got a motion picture contract with the Warner Brothers, changed her name, next thing you know she's stickin' her hands an' feet in the wet cement over at Graumanns Chinese. So one day, after seein' my mug in the shiny end of a spade I thought, maybe I could take the pageant route to fame and fortune too. 'Cause if Mary Frances Reynolds could do it, Debbie Reynolds! Then why not Peggy Ann Douglas from rural route two Caledonia. So, my thinkin' was…

*Suspenseful fiddle music.*

If I could enter an' win some o' them smaller pageants first like Miss Furrow o' the Plough, Miss Sweet Potato, Miss…Queen o' the Grand River Pork Producers' Association, then I'd qualify for the biggest, most important pageant around! Miss Caledonia. If I got that one I could enter Miss Canada—pick up a modeling contract, an' save up my money for my bigger, fatter move to Hollywood California where, just like Debbie, I'd be discovered, and be a big star!

CEC: Got 'nough stars in the sky. Wouldya look at that rain. Where's my pipe?

PEGGY: And anything worth chasin' has obstacles in front, like...Dad. Cecil David Douglas, otherwise affectionately known as Captain of the Scottish Protestant Puritanical Work Ethic. Tall, strappin', pipe smokin' chimney of a guy. Farmer hands, farmer tan, unadorned in overhauls an' rubber boots. Eau de Cologne's pig, horse an' cow sweat.

HELEN: A girl can do anything she sets her mind on, Cec.

PEGGY: And Mom, Helen Douglas. Small, red-headed, waves like crazy and a smile to beat the band. Refined sugar she is. Always searchin', inventin' ways to make a few extra bucks.

HELEN: Ginseng's all the rage so says the *Hamilton Spec.* "Crop of the future" they're sayin'. Nice 'ta get in on that ground floor.

PEGGY: Her hands are like two small machines; they husk, they pick, they gut, they milk, groom, knit, kneed, sew, wash, plant, bake, birth calves an' foals an' brush the hair from my eyes.

HELEN: Don did real good with his Holsteins last month, got a nice big milk cheque.

CEC: We're not plantin' ginseng, or startin' no dairy.

HELEN: Ginseng's good for the diabetes, fighting the common cold, potency too!

CEC: Ack! We're Scots, we raise shorthorn for beef. not fer milkin' an' no Chinese herbs ta cure hysterics.

*Looking for his tobacco.*

HELEN: Times change my dear. Some folks even have indoor plumbing!

*She turns upstage, then back around...*

PEGGY: I'd do almost anything to escape, and any chance

I got I was eatin' books. An' books where people went places like *The Bobbsey Twins, Black Beauty,* and *Heidi Goes to Spain.*

An' I'd race to the movies because like books they took me places I only dreamed of.

'Cause I knew…

*Music in.*

…as sure as the lilac growin' 'neath this slanted window there was a life to be lived a ways beyond these clapboard walls, that muddy paddock, the narrow creek that fenced me in, past Onondaga, Duff's Corners, highway '54… even Hamilton. As sure as cows' "shit" an' roosters—

*FIDDLER creates rooster crow.*

## Scene 1: Douglas Homestead

PEGGY: Most mornin's I was always half way up from dreamin' before that rooster come callin'. The livin' room doubled as my room, an' above the fold-out I claimed a piece o' real estate with all kinds o' pictures of famous movie stars. There's Elizabeth Taylor in *National Velvet*, Roy Rogers, Dale Evans and Trigger too, and my favourite of all…Mr. Bing Crosby.

*FIDDLER plays "Red Red Robin."*

BING: I seem to be needing some fire doll. Find me a light wouldya?

PEGGY: Sure thing Bing!

*Out to audience.*

I never seen eyes so blue, bluer'n robins eggs at twilight!

*To BING as she lights his pipe.*

Bing! I'm thinkin' a' goin' out to Hollywood next week. Straight to Paramount on Monday, get tested on Tuesday, an' signed on Wednesday. I decided I'd be happy ta take small speaking parts with dramatic possibilities!

BING: Nice idea Doll, you might wanna consider takin' some acting classes, get rid of that "accent".

PEGGY: What accent?

BING: Same accent as all them other folks in Caledonia.

PEGGY: What's wrong with it?

BING: It's fine if you want to play nothin' but little girls from Caledonia. Say, what's your rush Tex, the sun'll always be shining in Tinseltown!

*Beat.*

Boy, that cowlick o' yours looks sublime today… like the cow himself was sent straight from heaven…

*She gushes and FIDDLER plays "Red Red Robin" out. BING disappears.*

PEGGY: Before chores I'd try and get a few pages in of somethin' like *Rebecca*, by Daphne DuMaurier.

*Reading.*

"Last night I dreamt I went to Manderley again. I stood by the iron gate leading to the drive, and for a while I could not enter for the way was barred to me. No smoke came from the chimney. The lattice—"

CEC: Let's go Red!

PEG: *(Distracted yet determined to continue.)* "—the lattice of the windows gaped forlorn. Then, like all dreamers—"

CEC: Need ta git to Hamilton by eight!

PEGGY: *(Yanked abruptly out of Manderley's world she explains for audience.)* Chicken egg route!

"No winding drive, no cheery innkeeper, no lawn stretching to the sea…"

CEC: *(Grabs chewing tobacco.)* Cows udders'll burst, cats stream in, milk all over the goddamn stalls, hell breakin' loose, might as well give it away, practically am, five dollars a goddamn can, then that Prime Minister Louis St-whatever his frenchy name is'll only end up taxin' me an' every pig, post an' beam…let's go Red!

PEGGY: Oh Mom, only thing I despise more than the chicken egg routes' balin' hay on a July day.

HELEN: You thank yer lucky stars you're not the chicken or the egg. You got a busy day ahead, long list o' things to do, you do the thing you least want to do, first. That way the rest o' the day's a gift.

*Kisses PEGGY's forehead.*

Off ya git.

*Brushes hair from PEGGY's brow.*

*Beat.*

PEGGY: We stoppin' at the Waldorf?

CEC: Haven't even started work an' you're lookin' to put yer boots up.

## Scene 2: At the Waldorf

PEG: Both day and night before the route were devoted to collectin', candlin', weighin', gradin' and packin' hundreds of eggs in addition to killin' roasters, broilers an' hens. Somebody's gotta do it. That was this teenage girl's hot Friday night on R.R. 2, murderin' chickens an' listening to the Hit Parade!

Come Saturday we'd work the route seven til eleven straight peddlin' our wares. Dad an' me looked like some weird version o' Bonnie and Clyde. Him with his cap pulled down over his eyes, tanned knuckles grippin' the wheel. An' me, this wiry, inept little sidekick, day dreamin' out the window.

*FIDDLER plays a small lick of "Somewhere Over the Rainbow" cue which is abruptly cut off.*

I had a list o' customers in my hand that Mom had prepared the night before an' Dad'd stop the truck at each house, slide 'round back, hand me the goods, an' I'd walk up the steps to the Mrs. sportin' the biggest sellin' smile I could muster for a tip.

*She smiles, FIDDLER sting.*

I'd collect the loot, hand it ta Dad and do it all over again, 'bout twenty times. Then we'd finally stop at the Waldorf.

*FIDDLER plays a bar of classical music.*

Not that one, the one on Main Street in Hamilton.

*FIDDLER literally changes her tune.*

Dad'd belly up to the bar, order a Black Label and shoot the breeze with his farmer friends an' me, I'd order a malted an' fries and bury my head in the *Hamilton Spec.*

*Gasp, FIDDLER plays suspenseful music.*

An' on this particular day sandwiched between a top news story about Lester B. trying to make peace in the Suez Canal, an' a delayed ploughing match near Cayuga, was a little dot of a piece called "Angling to Success, Local Gal Ends Reign". It was all about Miss Hunter & Angler 1954, Miss Ruth Ann Marshall of Selkirk.

*Reading.*

"Ruth Ann has been winning beauty pageants since taking the Red Feather crown in 1953 and Miss Fat Stock in 1952. A pretty, hazel-eyed blonde, her vital statistics are 36-24-36", ooh.

*Taking in her own humble physique.*

"A natural blonde, she shyly admits to tinting her hair. With the $250 in prize money she took dancing lessons then music at the Toronto Conservatory." Holy smokes!

And beside her picture was an announcement by the Hunter & Anglers Association...they were huntin' an' anglin' for a new queen!

Well, that was it! The first step to my starlit destiny. The end o'shovelin' shit an' gettin' gams pecked by churlish chickens! Enter an' win. Win place or show! Just like Dad's prized barley an' Clydes...

*Beat.*

It was still pouring rain when we got home the farm dogs greeted us as farm dogs always do—

*She imitates the happy, wound-up dogs.*

"Where ya been where ya been?!"

PEGGY: Mildred, Teddy, Lucky you get down!

PEG: I ran as fast as I could, through the paddock, across the yard, an' as I crashed through our gate an' in my periphery was…Reeford Dixon, milk truck driver.

REEF: Oh, hey there Peggy Ann, you l-look awful n-nice today…

PEG: I coulda been wearin' a burlap flour bag an' Reeford Dixon'd think I was Jane Mansfield.

REEF: S-s-sun's sposed ta make an appearance tomorrow.

PEGGY: Nice fer tomorrow Reeford, but I'm gettin' pretty soggy standin' here today!

REEF: Ha, ha, uh…look I was w-w-wonderin'—uh, w-w-wonderin'—

PEGGY: Reef, you fixin' ta finish that sentence? I'm itchin' ta get inside to see Mom.

REEF: Oh y-y-yeah, that's good, no, itchin' ain't no good, itchin's bad…like the hives, like I had once, whoo, everywhere includin'-—

PEGGY: Reeford, I'll catch ya later.

*She resumes running.*

PEG: Me an' the dogs made a beeline for the house, our tongues all flappin in the wind, Then I practically tore our screen door clean off the hinges—

## Scene 3: Helen kills a chicken, and learns of the Miss Hunter & Anglers Pageant

PEGGY: Mom, you'll never guess what!

HELEN: I never guessed "what" once so you might as well tell me…

PEGGY: Look!

*PEGGY shows her the article.*

HELEN: *(Reading.)* "Cayuga Ploughing Match Stalled"—since when have you been interested in binders pullin' and seedin'?

PEGGY: No…here!

HELEN: Hunter and Anglers are huntin'…send picture! Peggy Ann…

PEGGY: Mary Frances Reynolds—

HELEN: I heard more than a lifetime o' tales 'bout Mary Frances Reynolds lately. Nothin' more 'an a racket, like the midway at the fair. Milk bottles refusin' to fall, toy fish immune to bein' caught, an' if they do get caught it ain't nothin' more 'an luck.

PEGGY: It's way bigger than the midway, and it takes more than luck, it takes skill and talent…and maybe a little hair tintin'. This is a new world I'm talkin' about Mom, not just all this here, not just cleanin' stalls on 54! I just wanna give the world a chance!

HELEN: Why don't you give that pump out there a chance and go fetch some water. Urma called, her an' Murray are stoppin' by fer lunch. You go pump the water, I'll go grab the chicken.

PEG: An' off she went.

*Beat, as PEGGY is left in HELEN's dust.*

Blue cornflower apron flapping in the wind, waves wavin' loosely atop her head, black handled knife in her right hand. She made her way to the coop and stood still as a stone in the doorway. A determined butcheress she did a quick survey, scannin' and calculatin'.

*Chicken sounds.*

HELEN: —enough t'eat today, leftovers tomorrow…

PEG: Then she eyed her victim…

HELEN: Hello Henry…

*Chicken cluck.*

PEG: …and the crazy dance of death'd begun.

*Stealthy music as HELEN stalks, then stops…*

And just as I was raring to launch into another round of beggin' and pleadin' I watched Mom's eyes move from me t'out across the yard, to our outhouse, and back my way again.

HELEN: *(After some deliberation.)* Alright Peggy Ann, what does it take to give the world a chance?

PEGGY: *(Elated.)* It says, "must have proof of age and appropriate attire akin to the event".

HELEN: …well, there's that gingham, handmedowned from the Allens.

PEGGY: "…a speech, hundred words or less,""

HELEN: You'll pen that easily enough.

PEGGY: "An' an outdoorsy type skill", and, oh, a …"ten dollar entry fee"…

HELEN: Ten dollar entry… Oh Henry, wouldn't ya like a nice coat o' rosemary, rub yer belly with some nice fresh butter an' black pepper? Come here you devil, fowl devil.

*Grabs the chicken.*

How's that for your outdoorsy type skill! We'll find the entry fee in these birds. We'll get least a dollar each, more if I fatten 'em up.

PEGGY: I could never imagine Grace Kelly's mother killing a chicken.

*Picks him, he quivers, guts.*

HELEN: Knife in, straight as a line. Happy entrails to you. You pluck his pin feathers an' he'll be oven ready in no time.

*Beat.*

Now then, who's gonna tell your father?

## Scene 4: Honest days work. Peg and Cec saw logs

*This scene is done with great precision as PEGGY and CEC saw in tandem with our FIDDLER.*

PEG: …for the city dwellers out there, most chores you're either working livestock or land. Milkin', groomin', cleaning out stalls an' gutters, forcin' iron down pigs gullets, sowin' seeds, pullin' weeds. Hard as these all are they at least allow for your mind to wander some. But when you're cuttin' wood on a crosscut saw, you're part of a team, fer better, fer—

*Three saws along with FIDDLER then a glitch.*

CEC: Don't push it. Told you that last time. You just fall off a turnip truck?

*They start again.*

PEGGY: Dad…I been thinkin'…

*Glitch, they stop.*

CEC: That's a dangerous beginning to any sentence. You put yer thinkin' on the back burner, just ride it.

*They resume.*

PEGGY: Teeth are full o' bark.

CEC: Teeth are not full o' bark.

*They stop, then another glitch.*

Look, you wanna think about somethin' you think about gettin' this wood cut so's we can get on ta feedin'. Get an honest days work in.

*They resume sawing again.*

PEGGY: What's a dishonest day's work?

CEC: Eh?

PEGGY: What's a *dis*honest day's work Dad?

CEC: *(Sawing stops.)* You'd hafta ask one of yer famous friends in there takin' up valuable wall space. That Roy Rogers knows as much about cowboyin' as I do bankrollin'. Probly thinks two quarter horses makes a half. Don't get me started on Bing Crosby. Pretendin' he's Irish.

PEGGY: *(Sawing resumes.)* He *is* Irish! Just cuz Roy an' Bing followed their dreams, don't mean they didn't hafta work for it.

CEC: We ain't gonna get this tree cut by followin' dreams.

*Beat as PEGGY summons courage.*

PEGGY: Dad—

PEG: *(Confiding to audience.)* And I remember jumpin' in with both feet at this time.

PEGGY: *(Back to CEC.)* Show business is what I'm supposed to do!

*Sawing ends.*

CEC: Show business. Now there's an expression I never

got. *(Beat.)* Next time you're sittin' in the dark, gazin' up at that screen, mouth gapin' wide, you take a hard look at ol' Roy. Faker'n a wooden nickel. Dale Evans ain't no better, yodelin' her way across the fields…o' Hollywood.

Hell, you wanna get away from it all once in a while, escape a little fer real, get dressed up, take a load off… Pick out somethin' nice; white bucks n' belt, hankie in your pocket. Shave. Take a drive up to the Blue Haven for a dance, rye an' water, music on a Saturday night. If you're lucky you might hear some Hank Snow. See some friends, then home again you go. Not too late. Just a night out. Bust up the week, not a whole…life took over. Batches o' lunkheads an' lunkettes makin' gossip and weavin' fads. Gettin' paid 'cause their bones look the "right" way. Where's the business in that?

*PEGGY stands mouth gaping wide unable to respond.*

PEG: Dad…Dad I… *(Then she reaches for Mom.)* Ah Mom!

HELEN: Well, that's it then.

PEGGY: Couldn't we, just…lie, a little?

HELEN: Cordelia Margaret Ann, your father is a good, honest and proud man and if anyone wants to call the pride he holds for his work and family a weakness, then so be it. He deserves nothin' but the truth and respect, 'specially from his loved ones. He's got a lot weighin' on him at this time.

PEGGY: I got a lot weighin' on me too!

HELEN: Once the rain stops pourin' and the sun starts shinin', that's the time to bend his ear. For now…a still tongue keeps a wise head. Let's pack up, or we'll be late for Del's.

PEGGY: Del Tricky?! Uggh! What are we goin' there for?

HELEN: I'm helping her plan the church social.

PEGGY: Ah Mom, why do I hafta go, can't ya suffer by yourself, isn't that what Christianity's all about?!

HELEN: It'll be a half hour outta yer busy schedule, you can log it for yer 4H hours. Now let's go!

## Scene 5: Helen and Peggy at Del's

DEL: Alright ladies, what's different about the mantel?

*She walks to the mantel where her Royal Doulton figurines live.*

Give up? Allow me to introduce "Poppy Jennifer". Isn't she exquisite? Look at those tiny wrists, precious, and that creamy, white neck adorned with a simple strand of pearls and cameo.

*Beat.*

Of course you've already met 1910 Duchess Margaret, 1940 English Chintz Linda, and lest we forget lovely Starflower Elizabeth, but I find Poppy Jennifer to be the more refined, don't you?

PEG: "Del" Tricky, leader of the local Temperance league and also avid smoker and closet drinker of gin and tonics. But for company, she always put on a awful good show.

DEL: Chamomile, Helen?

HELEN: Lovely. Thank you Del.

PEG: In addition to Poppy whatzername, Del had more plates out for display than in our entire sideboard.

DEL: Poppy Jennifer looks so charming among the

Wedgewood, or is it too busy perhaps? Helen what do you think? Egg salad, Peggy Ann?

PEG: Del always cut the crusts off. Crusts off is the kind of thing people who live on the mountain in Hamilton do.

HELEN: What do you do with the crusts Del?

DEL: Hmm? Why, what the devil Helen, I toss them out. Meringue? Macaroon? Rumball?

HELEN: I was wonderin' if you might consider keepin' 'em for us, we could use 'em for our chickens and turkeys.

PEGGY: Oh jeez mom!

DEL: No need to be ashamed Helen. I should have thought of it myself. …You are all havin' a, a "time" out there? All you farmers…are havin' a real hard time. If only that rain would ever stop. If only I could cast a spell I would.

HELEN: I can assure you Del we are doin' alright. We're even thinkin' of plantin' some ginseng.

DEL: Ginseng… Now that's Oriental, isn't it? Like eating dogs, and water torture? Miracle Bar?

HELEN: May I use your bathroom Del?

DEL: What?! Er, why, yes, yes Helen you know where it is. While you indulge I'll just catch up with Peggy Ann here. If she behaves I'll show her my album of Queen Elizabeth and the Duke of—

PEG: Blah blah blah. As I sat squirmin' in one of Del's King-Somebody-type wing chairs I watched Mom walk pensively down the hallway through the sunroom then disappear into the bathroom. There was lots of "downsides" to our lopsided log house, but without a doubt the absolute worst was having no bathroom, on the inside. So I think to Mom, Del's place was nothin' short of a dream…

HELEN: *(HELEN enters the bathroom. Everything is a wonder. She runs her fingertips along the counters' smooth surface.)* Melamine…

*She looks at herself in the mirror, imagines the room is hers. She turns, lifts toilet lid, looks down at clear, clean water. She then lifts up skirt and sits.*

Ooh, ahh, that's cold! Like sittin' on a china doll. Ohh ah…

*Notices little black miniature man statue that holds roll of tissue.*

Hello, little coloured, man, jockey. Me? I'm Helen, thank you for asking. Why, yes, of course, we come to the Queen's Plate every year. My hat, ooh yes I had it made just for today, then I, I, the ribbon is pure silk, raw, silk, toilet paper, ooh, yes I would love some!

*She takes a piece, smells it, she "goes". Fiddle sting, wipes then finally stands, and flushes. Marvels at the water disappearing.*

Where does it all go?

*She looks at herself in the mirror. Turns taps on and off, enjoys the warm water that flows. Dries hands on a pink velvety finger-tip towel. In reflection of mirror notices bathtub. She turns, checks time on her watch, and impishly climbs into the tub. She stretches out enjoying its awesome length. HELEN floats, swims, dreams, when suddenly PEGGY bursts through the door.*

PEGGY: Mom! Mom! It's torture out there! If I have to listen to one more thing about coronations, jubilees and world wars I'm gonna croak! What are ya doin'?

HELEN: I'm having a bath.

PEGGY: There ain't no water! Have you gone insane?!

HELEN: Perhaps I have. But, uh, when you're used to foldin' yourself up like a pretzel in a galvanized tub once a week this seemed like a heavenly notion. You, uh, go say yer goodbyes to Del, I'll be right behind ya.

*Gathering herself…*

An' with all due respect to your father, I'll help you, with them pageants, as best I can.

*Beat. PEGGY ANN cannot believe her good fortune.*

PEG: I got straight to work on my speech for the Hunter and Anglers. Everyday I musta filled about twenty pages of scribbled observations and insights on the backs of feed sheets and recipe cards. I pushed that pen so hard til my fingers ached an' I whittled and massaged those words down til I found the perfect hundred words.

*FIDDLER plucks along as PEGGY "writes" out loud.*

PEGGY: *(Counting the words.)* My name is Peggy Ann Douglas and I enjoy an outdoor life. Twelve. My family lives five miles from Caledonia on rolling, fertile land bordered on the south by the Grand River. I enjoy watersports at Hidden Valley Park in Aldershot, and Rest Acres in Brantford. Many have exclaimed, "Peggy has a future in water". Uggh, forty four words…

*Beat.*

PEG: I worked hard on oration by readin' the *Sachem* out loud everyday, "Last night fire caused $20,000 damage at R.R.1 Middleport. Saved were; a wagon, a half ton truck, two cultivators and a rake."

*She repeats and awkwardly over articulates for diction and speed.*

…a wagon, a half ton truck, two cultivators and a rake. An' I read aloud some favourite poems by Pauline Johnson. I chose archery as my outdoorsy type skill an' I'd try and kill two birds with one stone.

PEGGY: Across his shoulder lies a quiver, filled
With arrows dipped in honey, thrice distilled
From all the roses brides have ever worn
Since that first wedding out of Eden born…

*As she pulls back bow FIDDLER makes bow straining sound, PEGGY lets arrow go successfully, and a fiddle pluck signals success.*

*Beat.*

PEG: There would be twelve of us competing for the title. The night before, Mom trimmed my hair then did my newly shorn locks up in pin curls.

CEC: That's two weeks now, steady rain.

PEG: Dad was supposed to be out in the barn feedin'.

CEC: *(Taking off hat, coat.)* Unless there's a change, fast, there won't be no plowin'for fall. Come spring we'll all be way behind. Grain and corn'll fall prey to mold. McBlain was sayin' they're growin' so desperate down there in Cornwall they're thinkin' o' taking a sickle to all the standing corn.

*He takes in PEGGY ANN.*

PEGGY: Heya, Dad… Watcha starin' at?

PEG: My pin curls was what. I could feel the spit dryin' in my mouth.

CEC: You do somethin' different with your hair, or…?

PEGGY: Nope, don't think so.

CEC: Hmmph. Musta grow'd or somethin'.

PEGGY: *(Changing subject.)* Couple broken salad eggs beside the sink there, huh Mom?

CEC: Since when are they salad eggs an' not devilled?

HELEN: Since I'm taken 'em to Middleport church on Sunday.

CEC: Ah fer chrissake…

HELEN: Exactly Cecil, for Christ's sake.

*Beat.*

Look, we could start that ginseng real small… beneath them oaks'd be perfect, that way we don't need to think about gettin' any kinda fancy canopy. We already got Jack o' the Pulpit growin' so we know the soil's good!

CEC: *(Washing at sink.)* We're not plantin' ginseng. Takes shade 'n time. Ten years maybe more, before you'd see a nickel.

*CEC heads to back bedroom.*

HELEN: *(Deflated.)* Anythin' worth growin'…takes its time.

*Turning to PEGGY.*

Speakin' of things growin' wild…hop up there we'll fix that hem.

PEG: An' I did. I climbed onto one of our old pressbacks as Mom got onto her knees and started hemmin' like a madwoman. My ears so clearly remember the sound of her fingers crashing into a tin of pins. And she had the uncanny ability like most farmers' wives to carry on a perfectly good conversation with a mouth full o' pins.

HELEN: *(With pins in mouth.)* That's it honey, turn left, keep still. Can you believe that Queen Elizabeth and Philip are in Ottawa. Goin' to try an' say something in English and French! Stand up straight sweetheart! Turn, turn, that's it, imagine, the Queen, so close to us, little more to the left…

*All pins now out, she stands and admires her work.*

There. Very nice!

PEG: I loved my new twill skirt and shirt set that Mom worked so hard on; a hunter green top, with gingham mallards on either side of the collar.

*Beat.*

This'd mark the beginning of Mom's illustrious costume makin' days. We told Dad we joined a sewing circle, and that accounted for the time away and exotic fabrics.

## Scene 6: The Hunter & Anglers Pageant

*FIDDLER plays processional, almost regal music as PEGGY stands still on bench and then slowly descends to centre.*

PEG: I stood there real nervous on the day; borrowed my first lipstick from Mom called "cherry bomb", put a dash o' bergamot behind my ears just because, an' a nice lady at the contestants' table pinned a number on my right hip.

*Beat.*

In the old days o' pageantin', measurements was everything, just like with horses and cows. Construction of head, 15 points, hair, 5 points, facial expression 10 points, grace of bearing—that's that toe a way down south holds everything up proper—10 points. But in '55, all of a sudden, everything became all subjective an' judges were encouraged to look for that essential, elusive beauty known as poise. Poise? Poise…

*She tries desperately to find "poise".*

CYRIL DIXON: Peggy Ann Douglas, number six, Rural Route two Caledonia please step forward for the question round…

PEG: A spritely, pocket-sized little man, Cyril Dixon, ran Dixon's Hardware, was our emcee…

CYRIL DIXON: Peggy Ann Douglas, what is one of the greatest challenges one faces when living from the land?

PEGGY: *(Improvisation of a flustered, try-too-hard response—beginning with a very hesitant "This Land is Your Land, an' this land is mine…")* I thought that went quite well.

CYRIL DIXON: And now Peggy Ann Douglas, will demonstrate for us her prowess with the bow and arrow.

*She pulls bow back, extra pull as fiddler also makes strain, let's arrow fly… A dog yelps! Fiddle sting.*

PEGGY: *(Gasp.)* I hit Cyril Dixons pregnant dog, Crackers! The incident stopped the pageant for a good 25 minutes while Doctor Baxter come rushin' in to try an' extract my errant arrow. The entire Dixon clan glared at me and Crackers now only has three legs. The catastrophe musta harmed my standing with the judges, 'cause when the winners' names was announced, I wasn't one of 'em… I come in eleventh, out of twelve. Number twelve left early.

*Beat.*

No crown, no sash, no bouquet o' flowers… Just my picture in the paper, standin' there with the other contestants, plastic smile cross on my losin' face.

*Fiddle pluck.*

It was a sorry ride home with Sherry Locke an' her parents. Sherry Locke had the brains of a barn door an' the looks of a drowned duck yet she come in third. They dropped me off at Middleport general store an' I changed in the rain behind a rusty cistern and then I walked the last mile home. The farm dogs greeted me as farm dogs do.

*Now with angry, tired energy.*

Get lost Teddy, see ya later Mildred, take a bath Lucky. Our house somehow looked more sorry an' crooked then ever before. I hated that lilac bush all of a sudden, an' I remember thinkin' how could life possibly get any worse…

MISS PRICE: Peggy Ann!

PEGGY: An' then, the next day…

## Scene 7: School teacher Mabel Price offers advice

PEG: *(Turning.)* Mabel Price, school teacher boarded with us for extra dough. Cardigan-bound from birth Mabel Price was as plain as water an' the personality of a frying pan.

MISS PRICE: Peggy Ann…I was reading the paper this morning at breakfast. Page eleven was missing.

PEGGY: That's funny. Must been asleep at the press.

MISS PRICE: Hmm, perhaps. Actually, page eleven had been torn clean out. I find that rather "funny".

PEGGY: I'm sure you weren't missin' nothing.

MISS PRICE: I wasn't missing…"anything".

PEGGY: That's what I said.

MISS PRICE: Nevertheless, I was curious. So, on my way into town I stopped by McCullough's and picked up a paper of my own.

PEGGY: You did?

MISS PRICE: Yes, I did. Took me a while to find what I was looking for, but I found it. Page eleven, Women's Section…hunting and angling hmm? And there was your wee, tiny face, mixed in there with all the other faces, standing beside that unfortunate girl who won the pageant.

*Beat.*

Put the water on to boil Peggy Ann. Conversation is always that much nicer when accompanied by a hot cup of tea.

PEGGY: I got stalls need cleanin' Miz Price.

MISS PRICE: I think those horses can wait a hair longer, don't you? I suppose entering that "pageant" was a design to help cope with that, "acting bug" you've been incubatin'? Let me cut to the quick Peggy Ann. It's poisonous, this parasite. Akin to a dead end street. A threadbare bridge, a path leadin' to no where. No security, no sense of accomplishment, oh yes, perhaps in the moment, basking in the heat of those hot headlights.

PEGGY: Footlights.

MISS PRICE: I'm sorry?

PEGGY: Headlights is what you bask in just before you get flattened on the highway.

*Beat.*

MISS PRICE: Nevertheless, you must feel a sense of something-or-other, what, adulation, from all of the clapping and hallooing, but, in the long term, the twilight, which, you must always keep your eye on the twilight of life, you will be alone, adrift, a rudderless boat barely afloat on the black, salty sea of life.

*Beat.*

And all this...because, of a "bug."

*Beat.*

Allow me to offer up some guidance. DO NOT... QUIT MATH! which, I hear you're contemplating with great intensity. For if you quit math you will be unqualified to pursue any type of employment that will make you an integral member of society. A nurse is one of the most commendable occupations there are. A secretary, a seamstress— *(Trying to get her attention.)* Look you Peggy Ann, as a disciple of God and Queen Victoria herself, I only warn you now as I care about your future.

*Beat.*

PEGGY: Miss Price, you taught us once that Lister Sinclair said it's the job of humanity to find out what it's all about, what we're about and what our surroundings is about.

MISS PRICE: Lister Sinclair was a brilliant mathematician. Peggy Ann Douglas, if you do not stop this beauty pageant folly I will go straight to your father, and make no mistake, I will wave that horrid page eleven right in his face!

PEGGY: Then I'll hafta go straight to the Board of Education, and tell them what you been doin' nights on the front porch, beside the hollyhock, with Mr. Ted Williams of Simcoe Township...then we'll see who's in the hotter stew!

MISS PRICE: *(Sputtering and drawing her cardigan closed.)* You wouldn't!

PEG: *(Summation to audience.)* And that was enough of a muzzle for the time being, but you always got to watch an angry dog. 'Cause as soon as you turn your back they bite.

*Breath in to cue FIDDLER.*

## Scene 8: Peggy distraught, begins to pray at her foldout

PEGGY: *(Kneeling beside bed.)* God in heaven hear my prayer, keep me in thy loving care. Be my guide in all I, in all I do, and! Ach.

*Shifting gears she moves to Bing poster.*

Dearest Bing in Beverly Hills, hear my pleas, my woes, my ills, I come to you now for your great insights to help me through these hellish nights!

*Moving upstage onto the bench PEGGY ANN becomes BING and prepares to sing the first verse of "Accenuate the Positive" by Johnny Mercer as our FIDDLER accompanies.*

PEGGY: Ah, Bing, it's so easy fer you, you got bushels o' talent, me, I come in eleventh.

BING: Outta what?

PEGGY: Twelve.

BING: Ooh. That's bad. *(He sings the secong verse of the song.)*

*PEGGY, exhausted falls onto pullout. HELEN enters.*

HELEN: Sweetheart? Are you awake?

PEGGY: Mom?

HELEN: You're right honey, need to give the world a chance

somehow, learn an' do things you can't 'round here.

*Beat.*

Saw an ad in the paper, for modellin' school. They teach you all about technique. Technique, to bring out your natural charm.

PEGGY: *(Sitting up.)* "Technique...technique". I bet "Technique" costs a lot, then there's gettin' to technique.

HELEN: We'll jump those fences when we get to them.

*Beat.*

PEG: An' I walked towards our ole west window and looked out at the brilliant moonlight as it bounced off the spokes of our windmill, an' then all of a sudden it started turnin' an' spinnin', 'bout as fast as the thoughts in my head.

# Act II

## Scene 9: Milk Truck Elocution

PEG: Mom dropped the ginseng campaign and started a whole new sales pitch with Dad on the virtues of milkin' beyond our table cow Dorothy. After a few weeks Dad'd had the biscuit an' decided in order to keep peace, he better fork it over at auction for a few Holsteins and get that milk flowin'. This was good news for everyone. Mom and Dad got a small milk cheque every month and I got a lift to the Hamilton bus for modellin' classes with Reeford Dixon that milk truck driver. We told Dad I was taking typing classes.

*Moving toward bench which becomes truck.*

By that time I also sent away for a book called *Conversation and Magnetic Personality* and I'd try out whatever I could on Reeford.

*FIDDLER plays "Magnetizing Music".*

PEGGY: How do you do today Reeford?

REEF: *(Trying hard to focus on driving.)* Oh, I do, g-g-good Peggy Ann.

PEG: Magnetism is having to emit magnetic waves out there and have others be drawn in by your success energy.

PEGGY: I am inclined to think that it is a very busy travel day on our roads, Duffs Corners is tremendously busy.

*Fiddle sting.*

PEG: Being constantly magnetic is real hard.

REEF: Uh, P-P-Peggy Ann?

*Awkward pause.*

Uh… Brennan's had that calf they were long awaitin'. Nearly two weeks overdue, if you can believe it!

*Pause.*

An' Erlene Dindel was caught twice listenin' in on the party line. She never thinks nobody knows, but they do. Everybody knows.

*Beat.*

PEGGY: Hmm. That's very charming and quaint Reeford.

*Awkward silence.*

REEF: I also been th-thinkin' about other stuff… All this finishin' school, well, I don't sees how ya need it, all this worryin' 'bout walkin' and talkin'. Heck it's just walkin' and talkin'.

PEGGY: Reef, I'm not gunna win any pageants the way I am. Nice o' you to say all that. But I need ta work real hard to stand above the rest. That's just a fact.

REEF: I ain't really talkin' 'bout those pageants. Frankly, I d-d-don't even sees how you need them. You already make a p-p-p-perfectly fine w-w-w-ife as it is, without walkin' around with a stack o' books balanced on yer hair. P-p-perfectly f-f-fine w-wife. F-for someone.

PEGGY: Reeford do you mind if I turn on the radio?

*She turns on radio.*

I really like this song.

*They both listen to "Blue Moon of Kentucky" by our FIDDLER as REEFORD nervously drives. REEFORD accelerates the truck*

Oh, my, Reeford, we're gonna have butter back there if you don't slow down!

*Now terribly distracted, REEFORD begins careening until he halts the truck abruptly.*

REEF: Peggy Ann, look, I, uh, I ain't perfect by any stretch b-but I got prospects! I don't want you ta change an ounce and I know it's called finishing school an' all but, uh, well, I think you're as finished as a girl could ever be. Boy oh boy are you finished. And I just wondered if you, with me, if you might like to go ta Greens' S-Saturday night, have a dance. You don't hafta tell me right now, you can call me on the telephone if ya want. Hopefully nobody'll be listening in!

PEG: I remember not knowin' how ta tackle this particular game o' chess. I liked Reef; well, as much as a girl can like a guy who gives her rides and hauls her family's milk to the dairy. Fact was soon after the finishin' classes were over I saw myself eatin' bon bons and sipping daiquiris poolside with the likes of Clark Gable and Rock Hudson.

PEGGY: You're a fine fella, Reef an' a fair catch too—

REEF: Ah, it's alright, Peggy Ann, I, I just got ahead of myself there. S-started pouring the milk before squeezin' the udder. Thought maybe we could just try maybe a dance or two at Greens' an' see what grows from th-th-there?

PEGGY: Oh, uh, Reeford…uh, I'd, I'm afraid I'd be stepping all over yer toes.

REEF: It'd be my pleasure..to have my toes,s-s-stepped all over, by you.

*REEFORD suspends a hopeful smile. Silence, and then PEGGY looks out to house as if for help. Our FIDDLER then rescues PEGGY by playing a classical music to usher us into the next scene.*

## Scene 10: Modeling School

PEG: The Royal Connaught Hotel on King Street East in Hamilton was one of those places inside an' out that had the power to make you feel like you were a weed in the middle of a bunch o' glads. I walked up to a horsey looking guy at the front desk. He had an eye that wandered like a sailor on shore leave...

MAN: Are you lost, Miss?

PEGGY: I, I just come from...

MAN: Yes.

PEGGY: What?

MAN: Where?

PEGGY: Huh?

MAN: You just "come" from...?

PEGGY: I'm, I'm— I'm attending the modeling school.

MAN: Interesting. Name?

PEG: He grabbed his clipboard, with his long, asparagus fingers. His one eye scanned the list, while the other was off havin' a party.

MAN: Name?

PEGGY: Hmmm. Rita. Hayworth.

*Beat.*

MAN: Name.

PEGGY: Peggy, Peggy Ann Douglas.

MAN: Douglas, Peggy Ann, there you are. Ascend the stairs, turn right, pass the blue hydrangea, fourth door on the left. Haldimand Room.

PEG: I "ascended" for the first time, guess all the other times I just walked "up". Blue hydrangea, Pearson room, Selkirk room, Kitchener room, Haldimand room. Inside there were 'bout twenty girls an' every type imaginable from roses to wallflowers. Then a few minutes after ten this gazelle-like creature appeared. She had this wide, smooth red lipstick smile. Hard to describe the shade exactly…not quite fire engine red, but…Harry Cranston's barn red. An' she musta been 'bout twenty five hands high, and she swivelled her hips like the Middleport barber chair, an' she was really emitting 'cause without even sayin' a word we all just magically formed a circle 'round her.

MISS HANDFORD: Welcome ladies.

PEGGY: Her voice was deeper than Dad's.

MISS HANDFORD: I am Miss Handford, please feel free to call me… Miss Handford.

PEGGY: Holy smokes!

MISS HANDFORD: I am your Patricia Stevens representative. (*Beat.*) To be poised, gracious and charming is the inherent right of every girl. Many attributes enter into charm and poise, and all of them may be learned and developed through effective instruction. It is my privilege to offer such expert instruction. Congratulations girls, on the beginning of the rest of your lives…as women. The Stevens School is designed for results. Based on the sound principles of good health, discriminating taste, and rewarding, usable techniques, we can offer a sure way of attaining and realizing natural charm, self assurance and of increasing attractiveness.

*Beat.*

Together, we will target areas such as: comportment; moving the carriage with poise and grace. Wardrobe, personal grooming, and vocal training to ensure a well modulated and pleasant instrument.

None of this will be easy. But nothing worth having ever is.

*Beat.*

I would ask now that you each step forward, introduce yourselves, and tell the group why you have chosen Patricia Stevens.

GIRL 1: My name is Hazel Ann, and I live in Hagersville, we got five cats an' I like to knit.

GIRL 2: Hi, I'm Fleta! I'm from Dover, home of the Rovers! Goooo Rovers!

GIRL 3: Marilyn Corner, Burford. I'm here because my mother thought it'd be a good idea for me to do something constructive.

PEGGY: And the girl just before me was from Jarvis, Ontario.

PATTI GAIL: Hi! I'm Patti Gail, I'm seventeen, I like singing, dancing, and baton twirling. I love burlesque and Broadway and I'm going to be a lawyer someday.

PEGGY: My eyes just about popped outta my head.

PATTI GAIL: Oh, and I'm here because I think it'll be a blast.

PEGGY: A blast?! I loved her. Her hair was like chestnut brown silk. Her eyes were like big blue quarters. She was magnetic, type o' girl that could talk a fence post outta the ground! We became fast friends, 'cause otherwise, I'd have to kill her.

*FIDDLER accompanies the work.*

We spent weeks in the barn rollin' our backs up walls, walkin' with books on our heads and turning, turning and more turning…

PATTI GAIL: That's it Douglas…too much pelvis Elvis, turn those thighs out an' square those hips. Breathe, glide and compo-ort!

PEGGY: I can't breathe, glide and comport all at the same time!

PATTI GAIL: *(Teasing.)* …now that doesn't sound like a pleasant, well modulated instrument! Remember what Countess Handford says, "walking slowly and with purpose, chin up!"

PEG: An' all the while we were gettin' the bad habits yanked outta us Dad was doin' the same thing breakin' horses in the paddock.

PATTI GAIL: OK Douglas, now walk and talk. Elocute!

PEGGY: The big black bug bit a big black bear…

*Improvise walking and talking, and we watch as PEGGY makes a gradual transformation from farm girl to the beginnings of a poised young lady.*

PATTI GAIL: That's it, Douglas, we're gonna enter 'em all…Miss Norfolk Fair, Miss Caledonia Fair, Miss Hamilton TiCat! All of 'em! Pretty standard stuff plus you gotta have a talent.

PEGGY: Talent?! I still have nightmares 'bout cripplin' Cyril Dixon's dog.

PATTI GAIL: What're ya sayin', you wanna quit, you wanna throw in the towel?

PEGGY: No, no, I'm just sayin' that I think talent's one of those things that only some people are just born with, and I ain't "some" people.

PATTI GAIL: How did Joan of Arc soldier on? What made Catherine so great? How did Nellie McClung fight so valiantly?

PEGGY: ...luck?

PATTI GAIL: Courage Douglas, courage. You know what that is?

*No response.*

It's doin' the thing you're most afraid to do. Now look, I got a list o' talents in my bean that you can choose to muster up the courage to do or not. All ya gotta do is pick one and we'll learn it together. If you're not in just say so an' I'll be on the first bus back to Jarvis leavin' ya in my dust. You in?

PEGGY: Yeah...

PATTI GAIL: I can't hear you Douglas.

PEGGY: Yes!

PATTI GAIL: Alrighty. here we go...Hula dancing, pigeon training, suit case packin', table settin', hair braidin'...

PEG : We opted for the very traditional singin' dancin' an' baton twirling. Everything was "we", an' anything was possible.

*Beat.*

When we finally parted weeks later Patti Gail gave me a real pretty light blue diary. On the inside cover she wrote "…what's the point of always bein' down on the ground, when you can be flyin' high in the air." *National Velvet*. I gave her a picture I had took of the two of us. I held the camera out in front as we sat on the fence that wrapped around the horse paddock. It was sunny, and beautiful, and you could see the lilac in behind. I wrote on the back "Here's to us", and that, "the lilacs meant hope."

*Beat.*

## Scene 11: Peggy in the barn with Ms. Price (The Old Maid's Revenge)

PEG: I practiced everyday in the barn wherever Dad wasn't. Our clydes, cats, pigs and chickens were all more cultured than most people on Rural Route 2.

*Beat.*

And then one dark Wednesday—

MISS PRICE: *(Swinging the barn door wide.)* Morning, Peggy Ann. I have some news. Mr Ted Williams of Simcoe Township has proposed and I have accepted.

PEGGY: Congratulations.

MISS PRICE: Yes, and so you see,you won't be needin' to go to the Board of Education to report upon my conduct as I'll be leaving the school within the month.

PEGGY: Goody for you.

MISS PRICE: And therefore, young lady, I now feel the necessity, my duty really, to go straight to your father and tell him all about the finishing school, the pageants and your infinite deception.

PEGGY: Ms. Price! Please! The Caledonia Fair is in days! Mom already made the dress, we paid the entry— You wouldn't!

MISS PRICE: One day…you'll thank me for it.

*Beat.*

PEGGY: Sooner or later, an angry dog bites.

*Light shift to darkness.*

CEC: Red! Red! Get in this house right now!

*Light rises on CECIL as he walks downstage to confront PEGGY ANN.*

Thought we already talked about this business.

PEGGY: Dad, please! The Caledonia Fair, I can't pull out now!

CEC: We got Clydes we're showin' at that fair. You think I wouldn't find out somehow?! Paradin' around in a swimsuit in front of a bunch of fat cat businessmen so's they can decide how many hands high they likes yer legs?!

PEGGY: It's more an' that! We already paid the entry fee, Mom made the dress, an' I been practicing so hard!

CEC: You call playing at bein' somethin' you're not, hard?

PEGGY: It's not playin'. It's what I am!

*Beat.*

CEC: Where'd ya get that entry?

*Pause.*

An' how much? Five, ten—

*HELEN appears.*

HELEN: Fifteen dollar, Cecil.

*Beat.*

Babysittin', darning, preserves, oilin' the schoolhouse floor...fat chickens too.

*Beat.*

PEG: I don't remember much after that. Dad flew off to the barn an' I cried and screamed a lot, beat my pillow, and couldn't eat my dinner for the hole I felt in my stomach from all the hurt I felt. In one split second I saw all my dreams slip down the hole of our outhouse, everything I ever wanted! kerblewy. I took a good hard look around that night. The clothes I was wearin', the tired knick knacks, the news that served as wallpaper. An' that pile o' postcards Mom saved from places other people went.

*Beat, and then shift to HELEN and CECIL.*

## Scene 12: Helen and Cec

HELEN: You gotta let her go.

CEC: That's not what it's about.

HELEN: Oh, I think it is.

CEC: I need some time.

HELEN: There ain't no more time. She's on her own path, whether it be the right one is not for us to decide.

CEC: Seems irresponsible, crazy almost.

*Beat.*

HELEN: All of us here are dependin' every day on the sun an' the rain. The *weather* for goodness sake! What could seem more crazy or irresponsible than that?

*Beat.*

Cec?

*He is silent. Sullen.*

HELEN: I'll take her then. I will take her.

*Beat.*

We don't bend with the wind, we break.

## Scene 13: Miss Caledonia Pageant

BILL DEVERALL: *(At breakneck speed.)* Welcome one and all to the 9th annual Miss Caledonia pageant. Please welcome your twenty contestants from the Haldimand Norfolk and Brant County areas. Give 'em a wave gals!

PEG: Mr. Bill Deverall was our emcee for the event. He was an auctioneer by day.

BILL DEVERALL: Today three of our young ladies will walk away with prizes for their hard earned efforts, and she who is crowned Miss Caledonia will wear home this handsome silver plated tiara donated to us by Young and Sons Jewelers, Young & Sons, something for everyone, every occasion! Our lucky Miss will also wear the sash of Miss Caledonia, and be awarded…one hundred dollars!

*Beat.*

Making a special appearance today will be Canada's own Country Gentleman, Mr. Tommy Hunter! A little later on our gals will have the chance to have a picture taken with Tommy! Our twenty contestants will be judged on poise 'n grace, beauty of visage an' figure, talent and interview. Flash photography is permitted. An' now without further ado, let's meet our bevy of beauties…

PEG: And we introduced ourselves an' we catwalked, we pivoted, and…emitted whatever we could.

BILL DEVERALL: Sharon Bannon, from Brantford, the telephone city. Please name for us a political figure that you admire.

SHARON BANNON: So, like, not someone…we know…?

BILL DEVERALL: Laura Dunbar from Burford, sister city to Brantford. As a child, what was your favourite game or sport?

LAURA DUNBAR: Why, the hula hoop Mr. Deverall, 'cause it's so fun, an' you can't lose!

BILL DEVERALL: Thank you Laura. And now from Jarvis Ontario, Miss Patti Gail. Patti Gail please name for us an historical figure that you think the most of.

PATTI GAIL: Most of…I'm not even sure what that means, someone I think the most of. I would have to say the Famous Five, who in 1927 asked the Supreme Court "are women persons?" To which the court responded "women are not qualified persons". The case became known as the Persons Case. These great gals from Alberta fought for the freedom all of us Canadian women have today. They had what Lucy Maud Montgomery called gumption.

*Beat.*

There, she's an "historical figure" I think "the most of".

*She thrusts the mic back into his hands.*

BILL DEVERALL: *(Dumbfounded, clears throat, takes a sip of water.)* Thank, you, uh, Patti Gail. Patti Gail, from Jarvis Ontario.

*Beat.*

And now Peggy Ann Douglas, rural route 2 Caledonia, would you please share with us a most treasured memory.

PEGGY: Most treasured memory? Ah. Oh.

*Beat.*

Two years ago on our farm all our family was together, and we had just finished up Christmas supper, an' the kitchen was nice 'cause the wood stove was burnin'. Mom was gratin' ginger for tea, an' Dad had just gone out to the barn to check on one of our Clydes, Bonnie. She was a way overdue.

*Beat.*

Then, dad had figured the time had come! So he hollered for us all to some and help. So Mom, Aunt Rachel, Uncle Dave, the schoolteacher who was boardin' with us at the time, we all sprung up from the table, put on our rubber boots and coats on, an' we high tailed it. An' that foal she was comin' out, feet an' head first, which is what you want, Dad told me to grab a rope hangin' close to the bridles an' to tie it tight 'round her legs . Dad I— *(PEGGY ANN loses herself in the memory, and then catches herself.)* I had never done noth—anything like that before. I pulled, an pulled, hard's I could, she must've been twice me, at 'bout a hundred an' sixty pounds givertake. She made it. An' we cleaned her all up an' wrapped her in a wool blanket. Mom named her Ginger, and Dad told me I did a real, really good job.

*Beat.*

PEG: I looked out into the crowd…and it was a sea o' plaid. And there was Reef an' our dogs an' Mom…

*Beat.*

And on the other side o' Mom was…Dad. Our eyes met. He smiled at me.

PEGGY: And that, Mr. Deverall would be a real treasured memory…on the farm.

*The FIDDLER decides to thrust us out of the moment and directs us into the Talent portion. PEGGY hesitantly begins to bend and sway then eventually sings and twirls her baton to "I've Been Everywhere" by Hank Snow.*

Talent.

*She sings "I've Been Everywhere."*

*A shift in light, energy and music as everything appears to be dreamlike and in slow motion almost. Each runner-up passes PEGGY ANN.*

BILL DEVERALL: Our second runner up today from Burford Ontario, Miss Laura Dunbar.

*Beat.*

Yer first runner up…di-rect from Jarvis, Miss Patti Gail.

PEG: And she collected her prize calm and cool, like a lady…smilin', and winkin' back at me.

BILL DEVERALL: And ladies and gentlemen…your Miss Caledonia for 1956. Miss…Peggy Ann Douglas!

PEG: Crash!

*PEGGY reacts, lights shift reminiscent of shift at top of show to very bright, and then a beat.*

That windmill was built way before I got here, an' like the Grand River an' the moon an' the sun, it always seemed to be watchin' over us all everyday an' night as we'd go about our business no matter how plain. Some hours it just seem to stand so still, just staring at us in wonder or amazement... Other times it'd spin so fast like it might be laughin' at us or tryin' to tell us somethin' real important.

*Beat.*

I chose to leave on a day when it was at its most still. It seemed a good time.

*Beat.*

I didn't go too far, just a bit further up the river really.

BILL DEVERALL: And lucky young miss what will you do with your one hundred dollar windfall?

*Light shift, our FIDDLER creates a "waterscape."*

PEG: I took Mom to The Rose Motel in Niagara Falls.

## Scene 14: The Rose Motel with Mom

HELEN: *(Dipping her toes in.)* Ooh! It's too hot! Imagine honey, water that's too hot to git into. Turn it off now Peggy we'll waste it.

PEGGY: No Mom, it ain't no waste, not tonight. You could fill up this room, this hotel with water, hot water. It's all ours.

## Epilogue

PEG: I brought some lilac petals from the farm and placed 'em in the bath. For the longest time Mom just floated there, doin' nothin'...which isn't her way at all. Think she was dreamin' a bit I s'pose. I hoped. Then after a while, she started splashin' an' quackin' like the happiest, giddiest duck I ever saw.

*In this last speech, as HELEN loses herself in the bath, PEGGY slowly moves downstage centre almost becoming HELEN. She takes a breath and basks in the warm, bright glow of the light for a last time.*

*Blackout.*

*The End.*